SIMONE BILES
Making a Difference as a Gymnast

By Katie Kawa

KidHaven PUBLISHING

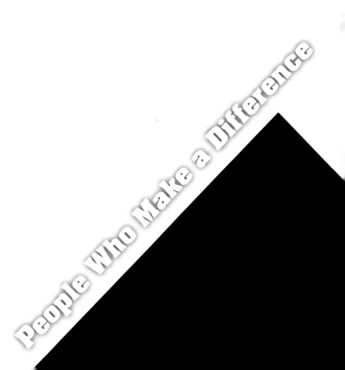
People Who Make a Difference

Published in 2025 by
KidHaven Publishing, an Imprint of Greenhaven Publishing, LLC
2544 Clinton St.
Buffalo, NY 14224

Designer: Deanna Lepovich
Editor: Katie Kawa

Photo credits: Cover A.RICARDO/Shutterstock.com; p. 5 Salty View/Shutterstock.com; pp. 7, 9 (left, top right, middle right, bottom right), 11 Leonard Zhukovsky/Shutterstock.com; p. 13 Kathy Hutchins/ Shutterstock.com; p. 15 UPI/Alamy Stock Photo; p. 17 Petr Toman/Shutterstock.com; p. 19 DFree/ Shutterstock.com; p. 20 dpa picture alliance/Alamy Stock Photo; p. 21 T.Sumaetho/Shutterstock.com.

Library of Congress Cataloging-in-Publication Data

Names: Kawa, Katie, author.
Title: Simone Biles : making a difference as a gymnast / Katie Kawa.
Description: Buffalo, NY : KidHaven Publishing, [2025] | Series: People who make a difference | Includes bibliographical references and index.
Identifiers: LCCN 2024010691 | ISBN 9781534548107 (library binding) | ISBN 9781534548091 (paperback) | ISBN 9781534548114 (ebook)
Subjects: LCSH: Biles, Simone, 1997–Juvenile literature. | Women gymnasts–Biography–Juvenile literature. | Women Olympic athletes–United States–Biography–Juvenile literature.
Classification: LCC GV460.2.B55 K38 2025 | DDC 796.44092 [B]–dc23/eng/20240307
LC record available at https://lccn.loc.gov/2024010691

Printed in the United States of America

Some of the images in this book illustrate individuals who are models. The depictions do not imply actual situations or events.

CPSIA compliance information: Batch #CSKH25: For further information contact Greenhaven Publishing LLC at 1-844-317-7404.

Please visit our website, www.greenhavenpublishing.com. For a free color catalog of all our high-quality books, call toll free 1-844-317-7404 or fax 1-844-317-7405.

Find us on

CONTENTS

THE GOAT

When sports fans call someone the GOAT, they don't mean the cute animal that's found on farms and in petting zoos. Instead, they're calling an **athlete** the Greatest of All Time. Very few athletes have been called a GOAT. Simone Biles is one of them!

What makes Simone so great? Some would say it's her skills as a gymnast, which allow her to do things no one else can do. Others would say it's the number of medals she's won at Olympic Games and World **Championships**. Still others would say what makes her great is her bravery—both on the mat and off.

In Her Words

"The word 'champion' used to just mean being on top or breaking records ... Now it means being vulnerable [open], showing your inner strength, being courageous [brave]."

— Interview with *Good Housekeeping* magazine from September 2022

Simone Biles has to be brave to do the flips, twists, and other moves she completes as a gymnast. In fact, she has moves named after her because they're so hard no one did them before her! However, she's also shown her bravery by talking openly about her **mental** health, hard times in her life, and problems she sees in the world around her.

FROM FOSTER CARE TO FAMILY

Simone didn't have an easy childhood. She was born on March 14, 1997, in Columbus, Ohio. Simone's mother couldn't take care of her children, so Simone and her siblings were put into the foster care system. This is a system in which children are taken from their parents because their parents can't care for them and are sent to live with other adults, known as foster parents.

Simone's grandfather, Ron, and his wife, Nellie, wanted to help. In 2003, they adopted Simone and her younger sister Adria. That year, while living with them near Houston, Texas, Simone discovered gymnastics for the first time.

In Her Words

"They [young girls] can do anything they set their minds to … I want them to remember that."

— Interview with *Good Housekeeping* magazine from September 2022

Simone was older than many kids are when they try gymnastics for the first time. However, she had a natural talent for the sport, so she was a fast learner!

AN ALL-AROUND CHAMPION

Only 10 years after Simone discovered gymnastics, she became the top female gymnast in the world. In 2013, she won the all-around title at the USA Gymnastics National Championship and at the World Championships. She was the first Black woman to be named the World all-around champion.

That was just the beginning for Simone! As of early 2024, she's won the U.S. all-around title eight times—in 2013, 2014, 2015, 2016, 2018, 2019, 2021, and 2023. She's also won the World all-around title six times—in 2013, 2014, 2015, 2018, 2019, and 2023.

In Her Words

"Growing up, I didn't see very many Black gymnasts … So whenever I did, I felt really **inspired** to go out there and want to be as good as them."

— Interview with *Vogue* magazine from July 2020

floor exercise

balance beam

uneven bars

In women's artistic gymnastics, gymnasts **compete** in four events that show off different skills. The gymnast with the highest combined scores from those events wins the all-around gold medal. Simone has won medals in individual events too. In fact, she holds the record for most World Championship medals!

vault

9

OLYMPIC SUCCESS

In 2016, Simone traveled to Rio de Janeiro, Brazil, to compete in her first Olympic Games. She helped Team USA win a gold medal in the team all-around event. That wasn't Simone's only medal, though! She won gold medals for the floor exercise and vault, and she also won gold in the individual all-around event. She added a bronze medal for the balance beam too.

Later that year, Simone came out with a book about her life, called *Courage to Soar: A Body in Motion, A Life in Balance*. In 2017, she competed on the TV show *Dancing with the Stars*.

In Her Words

"I'm not the next Usain Bolt or Michael Phelps [two male Olympic champions]. I'm the first Simone Biles."

— Interview with reporters after winning the all-around gold medal at the 2016 Olympics

Simone's success at the 2016 Olympics made her a superstar! Kids across the country wanted to be just like her.

LIVING WITH ADHD

Simone had many new fans after the 2016 Olympics, but she found out there are also unfair things that sometimes come with success. A hacker—someone who illegally gets into a computer system—shared that Simone was taking medicine to treat attention-deficit/hyperactivity disorder (ADHD). Simone's private medical **information** had been shared with the world, but she used that moment to help others.

Simone wrote on Twitter (now called X) that "having ADHD, and taking medicine for it is nothing to be **ashamed** of [and] nothing that I'm afraid to let people know." By being open about this, she helped other people with ADHD feel less alone.

> ## In Her Words
> "If you take care of your mental well-being first, the rest will fall into place."
>
> — Interview with *The Cut* website from September 2021

People with ADHD often have a hard time paying attention, being still, and controlling their behavior, or the way they act. Sports such as gymnastics can be helpful for kids with ADHD. Simone had called ADHD a superpower!

THE TWISTIES

Simone's next trip to the Olympics came in 2021. Those Olympic Games were supposed to be held in 2020, but they were pushed back because of the **COVID-19 pandemic**. They were held in Tokyo, Japan, and many fans were excited to see if Simone could have as much success in Tokyo as she did in Rio de Janeiro.

During the team event, Simone dealt with what gymnasts call "the twisties." This makes it hard for a gymnast to know where their body is in the air so they can land safely. Simone had to stop competing for her own safety.

In Her Words

"It's challenging [hard] to talk about how you're doing mentally since it's an invisible injury — people can't see it, so it's harder to understand, but I think that's why it's so important we feel empowered to open up about it."

— Interview with *Good Housekeeping* magazine from September 2022

Simone was still able to compete on the balance beam at the Olympics in Tokyo, and she took home the bronze medal for that event. She also won a silver medal with the rest of Team USA for the team event.

SPEAKING OUT

After stepping away from most of the events at the Olympics in Tokyo, Simone spoke openly about the importance of putting mental health first. She's continued to speak out about mental health and has been open about seeing a **therapist** and taking medicine to help with her **anxiety**. Many people believe this can help fight the stigma, or negative view, surrounding mental health and how we treat it.

Simone has spoken out about other things that matter to her too. She's called attention to the problem of **racism** in the United States. She's also spoken for women and girls who've been **abused**.

In Her Words

"I think of it as an honor to speak for the less fortunate and for the voiceless. I also feel like it gives them power."

— Interview with *Vogue* magazine from July 2020

Simone and her teammate Aly Raisman (who's shown here) have used their voices to support women and girls who've been hurt but feel like they can't talk about it. By bravely sharing their stories, they've shown others how to be brave too.

SUPPORTING KIDS IN NEED

Simone knows that she has the power to inspire people as an Olympic champion. However, she also knows what it's like to be a kid feeling powerless in the foster care system. Because of this, she's worked hard to help kids find ways to succeed.

Simone has worked with a group called Friends of the Children, which pairs kids with **mentors** who work with them until they're done with school. These kids have faced hard childhoods, like Simone did. Many of them are also in the foster care system. Simone has raised money to help Friends of the Children continue their work in cities across the country, including Houston.

In Her Words

"I've been a foster kid, so foster kids will always have a special piece of my heart."

— Interview with *People* magazine from March 2023

The Life of
Simone Biles

1997
Simone Biles is born on March 14 in Columbus, Ohio.

2003
Simone and her sister are adopted by their grandfather and his wife, and Simone tries gymnastics for the first time.

2013
Simone wins her first USA and World all-around titles.

2016
Simone wins four gold medals and one bronze medal at the Rio de Janeiro Olympics and comes out with a book about her life.

2017
Simone comes in fourth place on *Dancing with the Stars*.

2021
Simone wins one silver and one bronze medal at the Tokyo Olympics but pulls out of most events after struggling with the twisties and her mental health.

2022
Simone is honored with the Presidential Medal of Freedom.

2023
Simone marries football player Jonathan Owens and wins four gold medals and one silver medal at the World Championships, setting the record for most World Championship medals.

Simone Biles has continued competing for much longer than most gymnasts. These are just some of the highlights from her impressive life.

NOT SLOWING DOWN

Simone has found many ways to help herself continue to be the best she can be. That included taking a break after the Tokyo Olympics. However, Simone didn't really slow down. In 2022, she was given the Presidential Medal of Freedom, which is a very important honor given by the president of the United States. The next year, Simone married Jonathan Owens, who plays in the National Football League (NFL).

Simone returned to gymnastics in 2023. She won four gold medals and one silver medal at the World Championships. The GOAT's future still looks golden!

20

In Her Words

"When I see kids get super excited, it's inspiring to me. I think it's neat that I can be a role model by just being myself."

— Interview with *Vogue* magazine from February 2020

Be Like Simone Biles!

Raise money for groups that help kids in need in your community.

Take care of your mental health. You can do this by talking about your feelings, getting extra rest when things feel hard, and saying "no" to things that make you feel upset, uncomfortable, or unsafe.

Remind your friends and family to take care of their mental health.

Talk to your family and friends about issues that matter to you, and learn more about issues you don't know as much about.

Set a good example for younger kids by being kind and working hard.

If you're having a hard time with your mental health, reach out to a trusted adult for help.

If someone you know tells you that someone has hurt them, believe them, and tell as trusted adult.

Simone Biles has become a role model for many kids—someone they can look up to. These are some ways you can follow her example and become great at caring for others—and yourself!

GLOSSARY

abuse: To treat someone in a way that hurts or harms them.

anxiety: A mental condition marked by strong feelings of fear or nervousness about what might happen.

ashamed: Feeling as if you have done something wrong.

athlete: A person who plays a sport.

championship: A contest to find out who's the best in a sport.

compete: To try to win something that someone else is also trying to win.

COVID-19 pandemic: An event that began in China in 2019 in which a disease that causes breathing problems, a fever, and other health issues spread rapidly around the world and made millions of people sick in a short period of time.

information: Facts about something.

inspire: To move someone to do something great.

mental: Relating to the mind.

mentor: A person who teaches, gives guidance, or gives advice to someone, especially a less experienced person.

racism: The practice of treating others poorly because they are part of a different race, or group of people who look alike in certain ways. This word also relates to governments and societies that allow one race to be treated better than others.

therapist: A person who is trained to treat people's mental health.

FOR MORE INFORMATION

WEBSITES

Olympics.com: Simone Biles

olympics.com/en/athletes/simone-biles

This website features facts about Simone's life, news stories about her, and a collection of videos from her Olympic events.

Simone Biles

simonebiles.com

Visit Simone's official website to learn even more about this Olympic champion.

BOOKS

Hewson, Anthony K. *Simone Biles.* Minneapolis, MN: Abdo Publishing, 2022.

Loh, Stefanie. *Who Is Simone Biles?* New York, NY: Penguin Workshop, 2023.

Sabelko, Rebecca. *Simone Biles.* Minneapolis, MN: Bellwether Media, 2023.

INDEX